For further information, contact the Foundation for
Economic Education.

Find us online at:
FEE.org
Facebook.com/FEEonline
Twitter.com/FEEonline (@feeonline)
Contact us directly at: 1-800-960-4FEE (4333)

Foundation for Economic Education
30 S. Broadway   260 Peachtree St. NW, Suite 2200
Irvington, New York 10533   Atlanta GA 30303

ISBN-10: 1484970373
ISBN-13: 978-1484970379

Cover design by Esther Moody

The Great Hope

Essays on
Character and Liberty

Lawrence W. Reed

Table of Contents

Introduction

Some people worry they might look funny with a set of those 3-D glasses: one red lens, one blue lens. But when you wear those glasses, what looked flat before suddenly has breadth and depth.

When the author of this collection looks at the world, he's able to see things differently, too. Only his lenses aren't plastic and paper. He's looking at the world around us through two indispensable values. And when he wears his lenses, not only do things come into focus, they have more breadth and more depth. Want to try them on?

After a few years of writing a column for a small town paper, some fans of Lawrence Reed decided to put this collection together for your enjoyment. What's so special about this volume is not just that it's good reading. It's also that the author is, in many respects, having a conversation with the very people who live in that small town. Because they are among the people left who still hold the two values through which the author regards the world: liberty and character.

Newnan, Georgia is a sleepy little town and pretty as a peach. People who've known each other for years drink coffee together at the Redneck Gourmet, a downtown diner. They talk about the world's biggest problems as if they were theirs alone to solve. That's one reason why Reed writes about big issues in this small town column. He is writing for them but also channeling their values for a wider world. And that's what makes this collection as rare as both the people and the paper.

At this point you might think that essays on liberty and character are quaint artifacts that should be collecting dust at an antique shop in downtown Newnan. It turns out they are timeless values poised to return our country to greatness. The small towns of America are simply holding on to these values for us while the rest of country wanders in the wilderness for a while. But we'll need these values again. And they'll be there.

Why are liberty and character important? How do they relate to one another?

You'd think it would be unnecessary to repeat why it's important to preserve the value of liberty. If we don't value it, we'll lose it. It's that simple. We need only look around: Those parts of the world that value liberty least are those parts of the world that have created varying degrees of hell on earth. And those here at home who think there's a grand tradeoff between liberty and security, soon discover they'll have only gained another group to fear once that trade-off has been made.

If we were to unweave liberty's braid into three separate threads—economic, political and personal liberty—we could scarcely find a place in the world with all three strands intact. We'd have to be happy with one thread, perhaps two. And where there is no liberty at all? That is where tyranny lives. And suffering. But in those places where liberty still survives, you'll find peaceful and productive people by and large.

Liberty doesn't live in isolation, though. It can only thrive with its complement: character. A free people have to carry a heavy set of responsibilities: to work hard, to help their neighbors, to operate with integrity. Character means acknowledging and carrying those responsibilities like you have everything in the world to lose if you don't. Character means understanding your responsibilities can't be voted away. Character means doing the right thing even if there is nothing in it for you and no one around to see you do it.

One of the less perfect aspects of our democratic republic is that there are no angels in government. And yet if we are going to preserve whatever scraps of liberty we can, we've got to hold our elected officials to a higher standard. And that ain't easy. Expecting politicians to have character is sort of like expecting school kids to sit still. And yet there have been leaders throughout our nation's history who, according to Lawrence Reed, have been people of character—presidents like Grover Cleveland and Calvin Coolidge, and Treasury Secretaries like Andrew Mellon.

At a 2006 commencement address at Thomas Jefferson High School in Joplin, Missouri, the author had this to say to the bright-eyed student body:

> A person's character is nothing more and nothing less than the sum of his choices. You can't choose your height or race or many other physical traits, but you fine tune your character every time you decide right from wrong and what you personally are going to do about it. Your character is further defined by how you choose to interact with others and the standards of speech and conduct you practice. Character is often listed as a key leadership quality. I actually think character and leadership are one and the same. If you've got character, others will look upon you as a leader—not in the sense that they are eager to be subservient to you but in the sense that you are someone they admire and

freely desire to emulate.

But not every student gets this speech. .

I'll let you in on a secret, Dear Reader: The author of this book is the president of the educational foundation I work for; so he's my boss. But more than that, he's someone I "admire and freely desire to emulate." So he's a man of character and, as you'll see, committed to liberty, as well.

But even if Lawrence Reed were the sort of man who didn't practice what he preached, what he offers us in this volume is enough. Readers will not only be able to see the world with greater breadth and depth, but they'll also find guideposts in a universe that at times seems morally disorienting. They'll find sketches of people, living and dead, who are exemplars of liberty and character (and some who are not). And they'll recall that these values are not quaint enlightenment fancies, but timeless truths to be rediscovered from time to time.

- Max Borders 2013

The Deficit Americans Should Think About Most: Personal Character

From council rooms in small towns to the marble corridors of Capitol Hill, Americans are rightly focusing on ways to halt the tide of red ink.

Facing huge budget shortfalls, states like California and New York are considering radical cuts to balance their books. President Obama acknowledged the seriousness of the problem in his State of the Union message, calling it a "mountain" that could bury us and urging a five-year partial budget freeze. The president is right to admonish us about the magnitude of the problem that he helped mightily to exacerbate. Political leaders who are serious about fiscal discipline deserve some credit for finally acting to correct course.

But even the most aggressive measures to reform federal spending won't address the underlying cause of our public debt.

That's because the deficit that matters most is not denominated in dollars at all. Its currency is of the heart and mind. It's a manifestation of the values with which we circumscribe our actions, our purposes, and our values. I speak of a deficit of character, which arguably is the root of all of our major economic and social troubles today.

Your character is not defined by what you say you believe. It's defined by the choices you make. History painfully records that when a people allow their personal character to dissipate, they become putty in the hands of tyrants and demagogues. Such tyranny often takes the form of actual rulers, but it can also involve the serfdom of our nobler nature to a lord of lustful impulse. Decadence can destroy democracy as surely as dictatorship.

Among the traits that define strong character are honesty, humility, responsibility, self-discipline, courage, self-reliance, and long-term thinking. A free society is not possible without these traits in widespread practice.

How we subtract from our character

When a person spurns his conscience and fails to do what he knows is right, he subtracts from his character. When he evades his responsibilities, foists his problems and burdens on others, or fails to exert self-discipline; when he allows or encourages wrongdoing on any scale; when he attempts to reform the world without reforming himself first; when he obligates the yet-unborn to pay his current bills for him; when he expects politicians to solve problems that are properly his own business alone; he subtracts from his character – and drags the rest of us down, too.

Mountainous debts, unconscionable deficits, irresponsible bailouts, and reckless spending: These are all economic problems because they sprang first from character problems.

Reform starts with recognition. Not the easy kind that points out flaws in others, but the hard kind that reflects on, then roots out, errors in ourselves.

Is it wrong to take a dollar from the responsible and give it to the irresponsible? Of course it is, which is why so many of us decry the billion-dollar bailouts given to reckless but politically well-connected government agencies and private firms. Yet how many of us accepted taxpayer-funded aid when we fell behind on mortgage payments for homes we never should have bought?

We would express outrage at parents who, after borrowing heavily to buy gadgets and expensive meals, canceled their children's preschool when the bills came due. So why do we cheer for government "stimulus" that will similarly hurt our children? What is it about doing these things a trillion times over that makes it right?

Once upon a time in America, most citizens expected government to keep the peace and otherwise leave them alone. We built a vibrant, self-reliant, entrepreneurial culture with strong families and solid values.

Somewhere along the way, we lost our moral compass. Like the Roman republic that rose on integrity and collapsed in turpitude, we thought the "bread and circuses" the government could provide us would buy us comfort and security. We have acted as if we really don't want to be free and responsible citizens, so we get less responsibility from our leaders and less freedom for us.

The good news is that Washington's profligacy sometimes shocks us into sobriety.

In 1890, American voters raged against the Republican-dominated House of Representatives for its lavish spending. They punished the "Billion Dollar Congress," cutting the GOP roster in the House by more than 90 seats. A similar backlash occurred this past fall, when Republicans gained 63 seats after Democrats (with some GOP complicity) spent hundreds of billions of dollars we didn't have.

In both cases, voters seemed mindful of Thomas Jefferson's warning: "We must not let our rulers load us with perpetual debt. We must make our election between economy and liberty or profusion and servitude."

Heeding that exhortation takes more than punishing spendthrift incumbents in Congress once in a while. Our federal government is ultimately a reflection of our self-government, so Americans who are serious about fixing the country's fiscal mess must begin by fixing their own character.

Resolutions for reform

These resolutions make a good starting point:

• I pledge myself to a lifetime of self-improvement so I can be the model of integrity that friends, family, and acquaintances will want to emulate.

• I resolve to keep my hands in my own pockets, to leave others alone unless they threaten me harm, to take responsibility for my own actions and decisions, and to impose no burdens on others that stem from my own poor judgments.

• I resolve to show the utmost reverence and respect for the lives, property, and rights of my fellow citizens. I will remember that government money is really my neighbors' money, so I will not vote to loot them. I will stand on my own two feet, behave like an adult in a free and civil society, and expect the same of my children.

• If I need help, I will ask my family, friends, faith network, neighbors, local charities, or even strangers first – and government last.

• If I have a "good idea," I resolve to elicit support for it through peaceful persuasion, not the force of government. I will not ask politicians to foist it on others because I think it's good for them.

• I resolve to help others who genuinely need it by involving myself directly or by supporting those who are providing assistance through charitable institutions. I will not complain about a problem and then insist that government tinker with it at twice the cost and half the effectiveness.

• Finally, I resolve that the highest authority in which I place my strongest faith will not be the United States Congress.

August 22, 2011

Remembering Sam Tilden

If you're under 50 years of age, you probably don't remember the day when telephone "numbers" weren't all numbers. From the 1920s until the mid-1960s, most Americans with phones had "numbers" beginning with two letters that corresponded to certain digits on a common telephone dial. KL7-1234, for example, was read as "Klondike 7-1234."

My family's number was TI3-8597. The letters were meant to honor a man I never knew of or appreciated until long after the switch to all digits: Samuel J. Tilden. A strong case can be made that he was, as the subtitle of a recent book suggests, "The Real 19th President."

Tilden was born nearly two centuries ago, on February 9, 1814, in New York. After studies at Yale and New York University, he became a successful lawyer. A crusader against the corruption of the Tammany Hall political machine in New York City, Tilden was catapulted from the state assembly to the governorship of the state of New York in 1874. He quickly earned a national following and gained the Democratic

Party's nomination for President of the United States in 1876.

No Democrat had occupied the White House since James Buchanan passed the office to Abraham Lincoln in 1861. Fifteen years later the country was ready for a change. Tilden comfortably beat Ohio Republican Rutherford B. Hayes in the popular vote, 51.0 percent to 47.9 percent (he won Georgia by an astounding 72 percent to 28 percent margin), but a nasty political battle resulted in a deal behind closed doors. It awarded Hayes enough disputed votes in the Electoral College to edge Tilden there by a one-vote margin. Tilden remains one of only four presidential candidates in U.S. history to win the popular vote but lose the electoral tally.

Tilden was known for deciding issues based on what was morally right or wrong instead of what can get a politician elected and re-elected. "A great and noble nation," he once said, "will not sever its political from its moral life."

I've come to admire Tilden because he was firmly committed to limited government, sound money, free trade, and low taxes—which is to say that he'd have a hard time getting to first base within his own party today.

"Reform is necessary," asserted the Tilden platform, "to establish a sound currency, restore the public credit, and maintain the national honor." This was a time when the Democratic Party stood solidly for balanced budgets and for making sure the paper dollar was "as good as gold."

Tilden and his party supported low tariffs on imported goods. High tariffs protected Northern manufacturing from overseas competition, but largely at the expense of Southern exporters and ordinary consumers in all parts of the country.

Today, dozens of streets, townships, libraries, and schools from Wichita Falls, Texas, to Washington, D.C., bear the Tilden name. His home and a statue of him, both in New York City, still stand. But otherwise, sadly, the memory of this man who stood for liberty and should have been President is fading as surely as my old phone number.

The Futility of Class Warfare

For a country built on private property, risk-taking entrepreneurship, and respect for success, America sure produces a lot of envious people these days. Our expensive welfare state is fueled by the destructive notion that "greed" is when you want to keep your own money but "compassion" is when you want to take somebody else's.

We have a President, for example, who shamelessly appeals to the worst in us—namely, the desire to pull ourselves up by dragging others down. We're supposed to look with disdain upon those who have more and trust spendthrifts like him to seize our fair share of it, which really translates to whatever he wants to swipe and squander on his friends like Solyndra. No wonder all he can do is propose to divide up a shrinking pie—he's never in his life shown that he knows how to bake one himself. But he's just the latest in a long string of demagogues and snake-oil salesmen.

A few years ago in *America* magazine, Jeffrey

R. Gates bemoaned the fact that too many Americans have too little wealth. The solution, he said, was for the government to devise a grand plan, a national ownership strategy that will spread the people's wealth around according to some centrally planned formula.

Imagine that. The same government that can't manage its own fiscal affairs, that squanders billions of other people's dollars in subsidies for corporations and foreign regimes, that wasted trillions in a counterproductive war on poverty, that blew another couple trillion on silly "stimulus" schemes to fix a financial crisis it largely caused, should preside over a "national ownership strategy" for the American people. No thanks. We're not idiots (I hope).

It reminds me of something the philosopher Henry David Thoreau once said: "If I knew for certain that a man was coming to my home to do me good, I would run for my life."

Government deficits drain off more than a trillion dollars of productive capital each year. Taxes, regulations, and bureaucratic red tape keep many aspiring entrepreneurs from getting a start and employing others who need work. Welfare policies pay millions to stay in poverty. The government education monopoly spends a fortune and all too often guarantees that children are ill-prepared for a productive future. I don't know about you, but our federal government does not inspire any confidence in me that suggests it knows who ought to own what.

For starters, our "leaders" in the federal government have a knack for refusing to take responsibility for their own handiwork. They propose **A,** and when it fails, they propose **B** to deal with the problems that **A** created. **B**, of course, is yet another crackpot scheme, and when it flops, they propose intervention **C**, and on and on. Enough already!

A society can either create wealth or it can plunder and redistribute it. Which side are you on?

Just Do the Right Thing from the Start

When a politician offers you something at other people's expense, remember these words of the poet John Dryden: "Better to shun the bait than struggle in the snare."

Dryden's admonition would have saved us a lot of trouble if we had applied its insight consistently to our economic and political thinking. The failure to do so has produced one disaster after another.

When Lyndon Johnson inaugurated "Great Society" entitlement programs in the 1960s, wiser men and women warned that such programs would empower bureaucracies, waste vast sums of money, create generations of dependency, and bankrupt the Treasury. Unfortunately, the country took the bait and now struggles in the snare.

Just a decade ago, President George Bush caved in to those clamoring for a prescription drug entitlement program for Medicare. It's already projected to run a deficit in the tens of trillions of dollars over the next 75 years.

All this is proof of the value of core principles that are rooted in what's right, not necessarily what's popular at the moment. If you don't have core principles, or if you chuck them because you can't take the heat, you may pay an awful price down the road. Do the right thing now or you will inevitably regret your failure later. How many times does this have to be stated before its wisdom sinks in, especially in the minds of public figures we temporarily trust with the taxpayers' purse?

Economist Thomas Sowell illustrated just how current this issue still is when he noted,

> A recent poll showed that nearly half the American public believes that the government should redistribute wealth. That so many people are so willing to blithely put such an enormous, dangerous and arbitrary power in the hands of politicians—risking their own freedom, in hopes of getting what someone else has—is a painful sign of how far many citizens and voters fall short of what is needed to preserve a democratic republic.

Knowing what the right thing is and possessing the mettle to do it are two distinct traits. They aren't always present within the same person. It's character that makes all the difference. If you don't know what the right thing is, you lack knowledge that a book or a lecture may provide. If you know what the right thing is but can't bring yourself to do it, then you've got a character problem that only a personal change of heart can fix. Americans must decide if they want to be free, responsible, and independent, or handicapped with costly promises of politicians that put us on a path to dependence and bankruptcy.

In the end, Dryden's advice is a call to character, don't you think?

March 5, 2012

A "Visit" to the Crystal Palace

If you could travel back in time and witness a particular event or meet a certain person, what or who would it be, and why?

I've made my own list of such occasions and people—about a dozen in all. One of them, about halfway down my list, is a wonderful moment in British history: the Great Exhibition of 1851. It was the world's first great and truly multinational trade fair.

By the middle of the nineteenth century, Britain was the industrial "workshop of the world," producing more than half of all coal, iron, and cotton cloth. Powered by a relatively free economy that was becoming freer by the decade, Britain's railroads, factories, and machine technology were well ahead of any other nation's. It was time to celebrate not only Britain's remarkable achievements, but also those of free enterprise the world over.

Prince Albert declared that the exhibition would not be funded by government. Everything from the building that would house it to the exhibits themselves would be paid for by voluntary contributions, fundraising campaigns, and admission fees.

The project was in danger of being junked amid designs deemed too costly when entrepreneur Joseph Paxton came forth with plans for a monster edifice made of glass panes (nearly a quarter million of them). Thanks to the repeal in 1845 of Britain's window tax, the price of glass had fallen by 80 percent, making Paxton's design affordable. It completely enveloped the huge trees of Hyde Park.

When the "Crystal Palace" opened its doors on May 1, 1851, the sheer immensity of it made for a grand show: 1,851 feet long (a dimension intended to fit the year), 408 feet wide, and 108 feet high at the entrance. It was built to accommodate as many as 60,000 people at one time and nearly 14,000 exhibits.

To give every exhibit the attention it deserved would have required 200 hours in the building. It contained a 40-foot scale model of the Liverpool docks, complete with 1,600 miniature ships; sophisticated threshing machines and other labor-saving farm equipment; a knife with 1,851 blades; exotic fabrics and furnishings; looms; sewing machines; a prototype submarine; gas cookery; electric clocks; and one of the earliest versions of a washing machine.

The wide array of displays from America included a set of unpickable locks, a model of Niagara Falls, a 16,400-pound lump of zinc, a McCormick reaper, a Colt revolver, a piano that could be played by four people at once, and a violin and piano joined in such a way that a single musician could play them both at the same time on a single keyboard.

By the time the exhibition closed its doors on October 18, more than six million people had come through it. It was surely one of the greatest tributes to human achievement in the history of the world.

What the World Needs

More than twenty years ago, something quite remarkable happened in the little town of Conyers, Georgia. When school officials there discovered that one of their basketball players who had played 45 seconds in the first of the school's five postseason games had actually been scholastically ineligible, they returned the state championship trophy the team had just won a few weeks before. If they had simply kept quiet, probably no one else would have ever known about it, and the team could have retained the trophy.

To their eternal credit, the team and the town rallied behind the school's decision. The coach said, "We didn't know he was ineligible at the time, but you've got to do what's honest and right and what the rules say. I told my team that people forget the scores of the games; they don't ever forget what you're made of."

In the minds of most, it didn't matter that the championship title was forfeited. The coach and the team were still champions—in more ways than one. It's a story I've referred to many times because of the lessons it teaches.

Some years ago I ran across a few sentences under the title, "What the World Needs." Unfortunately, no author was listed, so I can't give credit where credit is due. In any event, I have edited it a bit and doubled its size with a few sentences of my own. The result is, I hope, a helpful statement about what the world needs if most of its problems—economic, social, and otherwise—are ever to be resolved:

The world needs more men and women who do not have a price at which they can be bought; who do not borrow from integrity to pay for expediency; who have their priorities straight and in proper order; whose handshake is an ironclad contract; who are not afraid of taking risks to advance what is right; and who are honest in small matters as they are in large ones.

The world needs more men and women whose ambitions are big enough to include others; who know how to win with grace and lose with dignity; who do not believe that shrewdness and cunning and ruthlessness are the three keys to success; who still have friends they made twenty years ago; who put principle and consistency above politics or personal advancement; and who are not afraid to go against the grain of popular opinion.

The world needs more men and women who do not forsake what is right just to get consensus because it makes them look good; who know how important it is to lead by example, not by barking orders; who would not have you do something they would not do themselves; who work to turn even the most adverse circumstances into opportunities to learn and improve; and who love even those who have done some injustice or unfairness to them. The world, in other words, needs more men and women of character—just like that coach in Conyers and the local folks who supported him.

April 26, 2012

The Liberty Factor

Once upon a time in America, individual liberty was a weighty factor in public discussions about proposals before Congress. We could greatly elevate the level of public debate today if we made liberty the paramount issue.

Would a proposed law have the effect of diminishing the personal freedoms our founders established when they pledged their lives, fortune, and sacred honor? If so, then that fact alone raised serious doubts in the minds of many about the wisdom of the law. That's the way Americans thought for a long time after the nation's founding. They took liberty seriously and they were skeptical about sacrificing it for the benefit of some government handout.

Over the last century or so, the liberty factor has usually been absent from public debate, or greatly abbreviated. We've given government the power to diminish liberty in exchange for all manner of programs and promises that the founders would disdainfully dismiss as "a mess of pottage."

An encouraging sign that maybe this situation is changing is the reaction to President Obama's health care overhaul. It's refreshing to see principled objections being raised that the plan is riddled with mandates and directives that would do violence to liberty.

A few years ago in Michigan, a private organization I headed constructed a new headquarters building. Not a nickel of public money was involved. I was informed by the contractor that we would have to place large, unsightly "Men" and "Women" signs in Braille on the wall space between two restrooms. That space was perfect for a picture I had in mind, so I asked that the signs be put on the restroom doors instead.

"Can't do it," the contractor said. "Federal law mandates that these new signs not be put on the doors, but on the adjacent wall."

The reason? If a sign is on the door and the door is propped open, a blind employee might not realize he chose the wrong restroom until it's "too late."

In effect, that requirement assumed that all of our nonblind employees were so stupidly callous that none of them would ever assist a blind person to find the right restroom. Worse yet, the origin of this regulation was hundreds of miles away in Washington, D.C.

When the founders met in Philadelphia in

1787 to prescribe the functions of a new federal government in the Constitution, who was it who added restroom signs to the list?

It couldn't have been Jefferson, who once said, "I would rather be exposed to the inconveniences attending too much liberty than those attending too small a degree of it."

Make an issue of this sort of thing today and you could well be shunned as someone who doesn't like blind people. Historically, this is how liberty is typically lost—not in one fell swoop, but rather one slice at a time.

May 10, 2012

Ending Corporate Welfare

Corporate welfare is one of the toughest nuts to crack in Washington. While almost everyone says he is opposed to it, Congress hasn't done much about it except to expand it in recent years with hundreds of billions of bailout dollars.

The Cato Institute estimated that direct subsidies from the federal Treasury to businesses big and small, cash-rich and bankrupt alike, amounted to nearly $100 billion annually even before the "stimulus" spending of 2008 and 2009. Companies often defend the handouts as being good not just for them but for the economy as a whole.

That's not an argument that was ever given much credence in debates over welfare for individuals. Most people seemed to understand that taking from A to give to B doesn't stimulate anything but B's spending at A's expense. Aid to Families with Dependent Children (AFDC) and other welfare programs for individuals were defended primarily as necessary and helpful to the recipients, rarely as a general economic

25

stimulus. Then came overwhelming evidence that these programs were actually harmful to the recipients themselves—producing lifelong slothfulness and demoralization, intergenerational dependency, and the breakdown of families.

It seems reasonable that what's good for individuals ought to be good for companies, too, especially since companies are nothing but collections of individuals anyway. Perhaps we'd be more successful at ending corporate welfare if we made it plain that it's only fair to apply the same welfare reforms to businesses that we apply to individuals.

Following this prescription, here's what corporate welfare reform might look like:

Declare an end to any and all "entitlements" to corporate welfare. President Clinton signed a bill that ended individuals' legal entitlement to federal subsidies. We should put businesses on notice that they are not owed anything, either.

Put time limits on corporate welfare. If we can't get rid of all these business handouts, then Congress should at least do what a growing number of states are doing with families formerly on AFDC: limit any company's time at the trough to two or three years.

Start drug testing for CEOs. States are moving

to deny welfare payments to individuals found to be abusing drugs. Taxpayers should not be required to subsidize corporate CEOs who abuse drugs, either, and there's only one way to find out if they are: if they're gettin' handouts, test 'em.

Require attendance at welfare-to-work counseling sessions. There's no reason why executives of companies that get corporate welfare shouldn't have to sit through the same social worker lectures that other welfare recipients endure. Companies should be cut off if they can't keep their executives in remedial classes taught by economists who can explain the importance of the free economy, property rights, and keeping your hands in your own pockets.

If you're wondering, would I also subject organized labor to the same requirements because of the generous handouts of money and power that they get from government? Damn right I would.

May 11, 2012

Homeschool Heroes

Of all the ingredients in the recipe for education, which one has the greatest potential to improve student performance?

The teachers' unions put higher salaries for their members at the top of the list, but teacher compensation has soared in recent decades, while indicators of student performance have remained flat.

Other answers include smaller class size, a longer school year, more money for computers, or simply more cash for fill-in-the-blank. But those factors exhibit either no positive correlation with better student performance or show only a weak connection. On this important question, the verdict is in and it is definitive: *The one ingredient that makes the most difference in how well and how much children learn is parental involvement.*

When parents take a personal interest in education, several things happen. Children get a strong message that education is important to success in life and isn't something that parents just dump in someone else's lap. Caring, involved parents usually instill a love of learning in their children—a love that translates into a sense of pride and achievement as knowledge is accumulated and put to good use.

Amid the generally sorry state of education today are heroes who are rescuing children in a profoundly personal way. They are the homeschoolers—parents who sacrifice time and income to teach their children themselves. Homeschooling is the *ultimate* in parental involvement.

Teaching children at home isn't for everyone, and no one advocates that every parent try it. Plenty of good schools, many private and some government ("public"), are doing a better job than some parents could do for their own children. But homeschooling is working, and working surprisingly well, for the growing number of parents and children who choose it.

That's all the more remarkable considering that these dedicated parents must juggle teaching with all the other demands and chores of modern life. Also, they get little or nothing back from what they pay in taxes for a government system they don't patronize.

In the early 1980s, fewer than 20,000 children in the entire country were being homeschooled. Now the number is in the neighborhood of several million and rising fast.

Some homeschool parents want a strong moral or religious emphasis in their children's education. Others are fleeing unsafe government schools or schools where discipline and academics have taken a back seat to feel-good or politically correct dogma.

Reports from state after state show homeschoolers scoring much better than the norm on college entrance examinations. Prestigious universities, including Harvard and Yale, accept homeschooled children eagerly and often. Homeschooled children make headlines regularly as winners of spelling bees and for other impressive academic achievements.

And there's simply no evidence that homeschooled children (with a rare exception) make anything but fine, solid citizens who respect others and work hard as adults. Have you ever heard anyone say, after a riot or a drug bust or a rowdy post-game altercation, "Oh, there go the homeschoolers again!"?

In every other walk of life, Americans regard as heroes the men and women who meet challenges head on, who go against the grain and persevere to bring a dream to fruition. At a time when troubles and shortcomings plague education and educational heroes are too few in number, recognizing the homeschool heroes in our midst is long overdue.

Energy
Know-It-Alls

Growing up, I was taught that wisdom begins with understanding that no matter how much you may think you know, there's still an infinite amount of knowledge that you don't.

That truth had two big effects on me in all the decades since I first heard it. One, it ignited a curiosity to learn more. Two, it made me humble. I realized that all the knowledge I've gained—especially about the future—is still no bigger than a blade of grass on a football field.

Yet all around us is no shortage of people who claim to know far more than I suspect they do or ever will. What's really disturbing is that many of these know-it-alls are so confident in their know-it-allness that they want to use the force of government to impose their dreams and schemes on the rest of us. Washington is full of people who are busy planning almost every aspect of our lives, no matter how well or how poorly they might be managing their own.

Energy is a case in point. An entire religion has arisen against fossil fuels and in favor of various "green" options. Its high priests tell us that we're running out of oil, that things like wind or solar or algae power are the way to go, and—here's the rub— we need subsidies, taxes, and mandates to get us there.

In the early nineteenth century, Americans used whale oil as their primary fuel for lighting. Prices rose as the demand for whale oil grew and the supply of whales declined (they were "common" property, not private, so everyone had an incentive to use them, and no one had much reason or ability to conserve them). No federal energy department existed to either plan our lighting future or regulate the problem into perpetuity. And guess what? No bureaucrat predicted it in 1850, but within 25 years, we switched from whale oil to kerosene, derived from crude oil produced by a brand new industry. Supply and demand, prices acting as signals in a free marketplace, entrepreneurs taking risks to make a buck: all of that worked beautifully.

Isn't this what happens all the time when people are economically free? Computer chips, satellites, and lasers replaced wires, transistors, and vacuum tubes. Cars replaced mountains of horse manure in our city streets. If we started running out of trees, do you think we'd have to wait for a government edict before somebody would think to plant more? What makes anyone think that government regulators, control freaks, and spendaholics know more about the future than do the real creators of wealth who actually have to solve problems or go out of business?

Maybe wind, solar, algae, or something as yet undiscovered will prove superior to fossil fuels. I don't know. But how will anybody know unless we let all possibilities compete freely? I can think of no good reason to substitute the judgment of short-sighted, election-focused, and often power-hungry government officials over the judgment of markets.

June 14, 2012

No Need to Make Voting Easier

"Isn't it simply awful that so few people vote? What we need are laws that make it easier to vote or laws that penalize people if they don't."

I've heard words to that effect many times, but I strongly disagree.

I think a much stronger case can be made in favor of making voting more difficult, not easier—a privilege to be earned, not an unbridled right to be abused. Election fraud is serious enough these days that voter I.D. is a growing trend in the states, opposed by the Obama administration mainly because the easier it is to commit voter fraud, the more votes the President's party seems to get.

There are those who want to make it so easy to vote that you wonder how anything so costless could be the least bit meaningful. Some years ago, I read about a Colorado organization called "Vote by Phone." I don't know if the group is still around, but the idea still is: allowing Americans to cast their votes on Election

Day by using a touch-tone phone from home instead of showing up at local polling stations.

Low voter turnout does not endanger our political system. Here's what does: politicians who lie, steal, or create rapacious bureaucracies; voters who don't know what they are doing; politicians who buy votes by bribing voters with their own money; and people who think that either freedom or representative government will be preserved by pulling levers or punching ballot cards or making phone calls.

The right to vote, frankly, is too important to be cheapened and wasted by anyone who does not understand the issues and the candidates. The uninformed would be doing their duty for representative government if they either became informed or left the decisions at the ballot box up to those who are.

Our political system—resting as it does on the foundations of individual liberty and a republican form of government—is also endangered by people who vote for a living instead of working for one. They use the political process to get something at everyone else's expense, voting for the candidates who promise them subsidies, handouts, and special privileges. This antisocial behavior erodes our freedoms by concentrating ever more power and resources in the hands of government.

I don't know about you, but I don't want these people to have it so easy that all they have to do is pick up a phone to pick my pocket.

Surely, the right to vote is precious and vital enough to be worth the effort of a trip to the polling place. Anyone who won't do that much for good government isn't qualified to play the game.

June 28, 2012

Media Report "Magical" Government Spending

The sins of the mainstream media, which lean so far to the liberal left you have to wonder what holds them up, are not so much what they tell you as what they distort or omit altogether.

Adlai Stevenson's description of the journalist as one who "separates the wheat from the chaff and then prints the chaff" was never more accurate than in the April 5, 2009, edition of The New York Times. Adam Nossiter's article, "Louisiana, a Test Case in Federal Aid," makes lowly chaff seem like nothing less than the cream of the crop. I could have chosen any one of endless examples from the past week, but this piece from three years ago has become a classic.

Imagine a thief who spends an afternoon pick-pocketing a sizeable crowd. In a few hours, he's nabbed thousands of dollars in cash and a bag full of credit cards. He then spends a small fortune at jewelry stores and makes off with the loot as a suspicious citizen who recognizes him cries, "Stop!"

If Nossiter were covering this little episode, the story in the Times the next day would read: "A Good Samaritan yesterday gave several gem shops a big boost when he bought more diamonds than the stores usually sell in a month. The benefits of the spending binge were confirmed by no less an authority than the store owners themselves, who promise to hire more employees if the generous customer comes back regularly. An obviously disgruntled passerby attempted to interfere in the matter by shouting as the customer left, but he was told by an angry store manager to leave well enough alone."

Make these substitutions and you have the gist of the article that appeared in the Times: The Good Samaritan is the federal government, the jewelry store is Louisiana, and the passerby who tried to rain on their parade is Louisiana Gov. Bobby Jindal.

The Times story notes that the feds had dumped more than $50 billion in money on Louisiana since Hurricane Katrina. "Indicators suggest," notes Nossiter, that "dumping a large amount of reconstruction money into a confined space . . . has had a positive outcome." Apparently, not even the government can spend

$50 billion on construction without yielding some construction.

Gov. Jindal raised objections to this "free" money. He warned of "dire consequences" of the federal spending spree. But Nossiter says not to worry: "In Louisiana, the consequences have hardly been dire—just the opposite, in fact." He's looking at the few upon whom the money was spent and ignoring all those from whom the money was taken (including future generations to whom Washington is sending most of the bill through its monumental debt).

Sadly, the Times story is typical of what passes these days for mainstream journalism. Its reasoning is so infantile, its evidence so transparent, and its economics so woefully deficient that one can't help but wonder if it was printed simply to advance somebody's brainless big government agenda.

July 12, 2012

If Incentives Matter, We Might Be in Trouble

Theologian C. S. Lewis was a keen observer of people and the consequences of their ideas—good or bad.

He took note of our topsy-turvy world with these cogent words: "In a sort of ghastly simplicity we remove the organ and demand the function. We make men without chests and expect of them virtue and enterprise. We laugh at honour and are shocked to find traitors in our midst. We castrate and bid the geldings be fruitful."

So behavior is actually influenced by the incentives and the disincentives we confront? You bet it is. This is an iron law of the human condition.

The biggest advocates of taxes and regulations on smoking argue that such penalties will deter the smoker. Strange, isn't it, that many of those same people think they can soak the entrepreneur, the investor, the saver, the employer, and the inventor with little or no negative consequence.

The Obama administration says it wants to stimulate the economy but calls for higher taxes on those who take a risk, create an enterprise, hire people, or invent a product. It says it wants to foster medical innovation, then it imposes a tax on medical devices. It vilifies the rich and successful while imploring us to work to become rich and successful.

People respond to incentives and to their opposite, disincentives. An individual will feel compelled to respond favorably to something that promises great personal benefit at low cost or risk. The same individual will shun those things which would set his progress back, much as a hot stove is a disincentive to bare hands. Human choice is thus influenced by economic incentives and by changes in economic incentives.

Incentives and disincentives explain why higher prices call forth greater supply and why lower prices do not; why bad behavior never goes away if it's subsidized; why students work harder in a class where excellence is rewarded and failure is penalized than in a class where everyone gets a "C"; why some people quit working and go on welfare; why politicians promise more spending as long as voters re-elect them for it; why capitalist economies do better than socialist economies; and so on and so forth.

The future world we are creating will surely be shaped by the incentives and disincentives we are putting in place today. In that light, we must hope that this warning from novelist and philosopher Ayn Rand does not also become our epitaph:

> When you see that trading is done, not by consent, but by compulsion; when you see that in order to produce, you need to obtain permission from men who produce nothing; when you see that money is flowing to those who deal, not in goods, but in favors; when you see that men get richer by graft and by pull than by work, and your laws don't protect you against them, but protect them against you; when you see corruption being rewarded and honesty becoming a self-sacrifice—you may know that your society is doomed.

Limit Government to Maximize Freedom

Those of us who want to make government small and keep it limited as America's founders intended sometimes come across to others as naysayers.

Because we don't fall for the promises of politicians to take care of every corner of our lives, we get accused of being mean and uncaring. But we should be quick to point out we are opposed to excessive government because we are in favor of some very positive, important things. We want to limit government ultimately because we support freedom, without which life would hardly be worth living.

We want to limit government because we want to maximize opportunity, enterprise, and creativity. We want to permit individuals to go as far as their talents, ambitions, and industry can take them. We want to limit government because we want people to dream and have the room to bring those dreams to fruition, for themselves and their families.

We want to limit government because we want to strengthen other institutions of civil society that tend to shrink as government grows—institutions such as the family, church, community, and the many voluntary associations that form the bedrock of American liberty, prosperity, and self-reliance.

And we want to limit government because we've learned something from the thousands of years of experience with it—enough to know that it ought properly to be confined to certain minimal but critical functions and otherwise leave us alone.

History is littered with the wreckage of government planners and their presumptuous visions of "the common good." They claim that to make an omelet, they must break a few eggs. But as they accumulate power, they kill or impoverish millions along the way. If Big Government ever earns a final epitaph, it will be this: "Here lies a contrivance cooked up by know-it-alls and busybodies who broke eggs with abandon but never, ever created an omelet."

At the core of our principles are these indisputable truths: Government has nothing to give anybody except what it first takes from somebody, and a government that's big enough to give you everything you want is big enough to take away everything you've got.

No generation ever grasped the meaning of this better than that of the founders. One of them is credited with this astute observation: "Government is not reason. It is not eloquence. It is force. Like fire, it can be a dangerous servant or a fearful master." In other words, even when government is no larger than what our founders wanted and if it does its job so well as to be a true servant, it's still dangerous.

Keep government small and keep your eye on it because it will grab whatever power it can get its hands on at your expense.

July 26, 2012

Union Political Spending Rests on Forced Dues

The Wall Street Journal reported earlier this month that organized labor spends about four times as much on politics as generally thought—about $4.4 billion between 2005 and 2011. Nearly all of that money went to support politicians who routinely vote to drown Americans—including workers—in taxes, regulations, debt, and wasteful spending.

But what union members get with the dollars their unions spend on politics is a minor indiscretion compared to the sin of how union bosses get much of that money in the first place. I'm referring, of course, to compulsory dues.

Unionized workers pay dues for their unions' collective-bargaining activities, but they are not required to financially support the political or ideological causes of Big Labor bosses. In fact, workers are actually entitled to a refund of their dues used for purposes unrelated to collective bargaining, contract administration, or grievance processing, according to the 1988

U.S. Supreme Court decision in Communication Workers of America v. Beck.

In that celebrated case, it was determined that the union had been using as much as 79 percent of Harry Beck's dues for partisan politics—and almost all of it on behalf of one particular political party. Nearly 25 years later, state and federal governments have done almost nothing to enforce the Beck decision.

Peer pressure and veiled threats from the top discourage the informed few from even attempting to exercise their Beck rights. When union members have actually challenged their union leadership to honor the decision, union leaders have routinely stonewalled, falsified the numbers, and forced disgruntled workers to spend large sums of money to litigate the issue.

In 1992 in the state of Washington, 72 percent of voters approved a ballot initiative requiring teachers unions to secure written permission from each worker before deducting political-action assessments from his paycheck.

What happened afterward was astonishing. The number of teachers contributing to their union's political-action committees plummeted from over 45,000 to just 8,000. And the number of state workers making such a contribution—over 40,000 before the change—evaporated to a microscopic 82. That's not a typo. No wonder unions everywhere are scared stiff that Beck rights might be enforced someday.

The same sort of thing has happened in Wisconsin since Gov. Scott Walker's reforms kicked in more than a year ago. Membership in AFSCME, the government employee union, has fallen by more than half since early 2011. Now that the union has to rely on its members' approval to spend their money on politics, few of those members are giving the union so much as a nickel.

Thomas Jefferson was right on the money when he said 200 years ago, "To compel a man to furnish funds for the propagation of ideas he disbelieves and abhors is sinful and tyrannical." In a free society, no union—indeed, no company or organization of any kind—should ever be allowed to force anyone to pay for its political spending.

The End of the Socialized Medicine Road

Two years ago, the mish-mash of promises and regulations known as "Obamacare" was rammed through Congress. Most of it hasn't even kicked in, but estimates already suggest it will cost two to three times what we were told in 2010. We're well down the dead-end road to socialized medicine, complete with mandates for "free" contraceptives.

What's wrong with socialized medicine? Twenty-five years ago, a friend of mine put it more concisely than I've ever heard it put before. His name was Dr. Roberto Calderon and he was a radiologist in Managua, Nicaragua.

Dr. Calderon didn't just answer this question with exotic theories. His insight was derived from the time when the Marxist Sandinistas ran his country and tried to put the state's bureaucracy in charge of almost everything. He saw socialized medicine from the inside and argued that it doesn't work for the following five reasons:

1. The patient can't choose the doctor.

The bureaucratic process ends up making the important assignment of which physician shall treat the patient. He who pays the piper calls the tune. Too much freedom for the patient makes life difficult for the bureaucrats, who already have more than enough of their own paperwork to deal with.

2. The doctor can't choose the patient.

Assignments are assignments under socialized medicine. Referring a patient to another doctor is an unnecessary complication, and it screws up the system. Because medical services are made "free" by the state, demand for them goes up, which means that every doctor quickly becomes overbooked and overworked. So, doctors receive their orders: Just get the job done whether you like the patient or not and whether or not you are suitable for him.

3. The doctor gets paid at the end of the month regardless of what or how well he did.

Even an eighth-grader understands why this is a prescription for high cost and poor performance. What in the world makes socialists think that people work harder and better for some faceless bureaucracy than they work for themselves?

4. The patient doesn't get consoled.

Dr. Calderon told me that it was common in Nicaragua in the 1980s for patients to complain that "the doctor hardly speaks to me; he just says to sit there and be quiet." An important, even vital, role of the healer is to provide comfort, reassurance, and a positive mental attitude to the sick. This role gets lost when doctors become short-order cooks in a government-run soup kitchen.

5. The patient doesn't get well.

That's exactly the way Dr. Calderon put it, but he really meant that far too many patients under socialized medicine are "chronically sick" as a direct consequence of the previous four points. People go on waiting lists and many of them die before they ever get to the head of the line.

But, you say, this is a worst-case scenario and surely Obamacare would never evolve into such a nightmare. Yeah, just like they said in 1913 when the income tax was passed that nobody would ever pay more than 10 percent.

August 16, 2012

The Attitude of Gratitude

Ever since Samuel Smiles wrote his remarkably influential *Self Help* in 1859, hundreds of books in the same vein have appeared in print. Twentieth-century authors like Dale Carnegie and John Maxwell sold millions of copies of their works, all aimed at inspiring people to improve their attitudes or work habits or personal character. So obviously there's been a lot of interest for a long time in at least reading about self-improvement, even if we don't actually do it.

I recently picked up a cheap, secondhand copy of a 2008 paperback by Dr. Robert A. Emmons entitled *Thanks! How Practicing Gratitude Can Make You Happier*. Emmons is a professor at the University of California and editor-in-chief of the *Journal of Positive Psychology*. At first, I thought I'd skim a few pages, glean a few quotable quotes, and then stick it on the shelf with all the other self-improvement books gathering dust in my basement. But this one grabbed my attention on the first page. I couldn't put it down until I read the other 208.

This book isn't just a feel-good collection of generalities and catchy phrases. It's rooted in what the latest science can teach us. In language a lay reader can easily understand, Emmons reveals groundbreaking research into the previously underexamined emotion we call "gratitude." As defined by Emmons, gratitude is the acknowledgement of goodness in one's life and the recognition that the source of this goodness lies at least partially outside one's self.

Years of study by Emmons and his associates show that "grateful people experience higher levels of positive emotions such as joy, enthusiasm, love, happiness and optimism, and that the practice of gratitude as a discipline protects a person from the destructive impulses of envy, resentment, greed and bitterness."

A grateful attitude enriches life. Emmons believes it elevates, energizes, inspires, and transforms. The science of it proves that gratitude is an indispensable key to happiness (the more of it you can muster, the happier you'll be) and that happiness adds up to nine years to life expectancy.

Gratitude isn't just a knee-jerk, unthinking "thank you." It's much more than a warm and fuzzy sentiment. It's not automatic. Some people, in fact, feel and express it all too rarely. And as grateful a person as you may think you are, chances are you can develop an even more grateful attitude, a task that carries ample rewards that more than compensate for its moral and intellectual challenges.

Emmons cites plenty of evidence for his thesis, but most readers will find his seventh and final chapter, a mere 24 pages, the most useful part of the book. There the author lays out 10 steps (exercises, in fact) for cultivating this critically important emotion. If I had space to tell you here what those steps were, you might not read the book.

So if you want a serious self-improvement book, pick this one up. I guarantee that you'll be grateful for the recommendation.

Detroit: The Greece of the Midwest

Bankruptcies by major California cities are making headlines these days, but it's a good bet the worst is yet to come. And not just in the Golden State. For most of the same reasons—corruption, public-sector unionism, out-of-control spending—we may soon witness the formal bankruptcy of a city once known worldwide as an economic powerhouse. That city is Detroit.

Perhaps no other metropolis in America has suffered more from destructive policies of government in the last half-century. Detroit's per capita tax burden is several times the average for the other municipalities within Michigan. The weight of its gargantuan bureaucracy and the extent of its legendary corruption are staggering. Locally, city services have been likened to those of Third World backwaters.

Barely 50 years ago, Detroit boasted a population of more than two million. After decades of flight, scarcely 700,000 souls are left, many of them trapped in poverty and enveloped by some of the highest crime and welfare rates in the country.

The number of people who vanished from Detroit in the last decade—about a quarter million—is nearly twice the 140,000 who left New Orleans right after Hurricane Katrina.

But not even Mother Nature could possibly do as much damage to a major city as big government has done to Detroit. For decades, the political establishment in Detroit jacked up taxes, funneled money to its union cronies, and regulated tens of thousands of private businesses right out of town.

No failure of government is too big to prevent that establishment from trying to throw more public money at it. The Motor City ought to be a showcase of modern liberalism because liberals have had their way there forever, but the wreckage stands as testimony to both the economic and the moral bankruptcy of their welfare state.

Many of those who left were "makers" of things; most of those left behind are "takers" of things. Detroit is the Greece of the American Midwest.

Detroit's public schools are among the worst in the nation despite spending nearly $16,000 annually per pupil. That's about 60 percent more than we spend on average here in Georgia. Dropout rates are in the stratosphere, and test scores are so bad the superintendent of the city's schools once said they were no better than if the students had simply guessed at the answers.

In other words, instead of $16,000 for each student, they could spend absolutely nothing and get essentially the same results. The school system doesn't exist for the benefit of the kids. It exists for the benefit of the parasitical teachers' unions and the overpaid bureaucracy that suck off of it.

The famous French economist Frédéric Bastiat wrote, "And now that the legislators and do-gooders have so futilely inflicted so many systems upon society, may they finally end where they should have begun: May they reject all systems, and try liberty."

That's about the best advice anybody could possibly give Detroiters, if only they would listen.

August 30, 2012

A Truly Remarkable Woman

A hundred years ago, who was the most revered woman in America? It likely was someone not 5 percent of today's population could identify if they heard her name: Fanny Crosby.

She was born Frances Jane Crosby in Putnam County, New York, in 1820. She died in 1915, just a month short of her 95th birthday. And what a long life of achievement it was.

She earned great fame and appreciation for her charitable work in inner cities, especially when she nursed the sick during New York's terrible cholera epidemic in the late 1840s. Thousands fled the city but Fanny stayed behind, contracting the disease herself but later recovering.

She probably holds the record for having met (and befriended) more Presidents of the United States than any other American, living or dead—an astounding 21, or almost half of the 44 we've had. She met every single one (in some cases after they served in the White

House) from John Quincy Adams to Woodrow Wilson. She was also the very first woman to address the United States Congress.

Fanny Crosby was clearly a woman that people wanted to meet. The reason? She was the best-known hymn-writer of her day. She wrote nearly 9,000 hymns in her lifetime, a record no one else has ever even approached. America's Protestant churches by the late nineteenth century were filled with music from the creative mind of Fanny Crosby. Some of her hymns are still well-known and widely sung today, from "To God Be the Glory" to "Blessed Assurance."

What made Fanny's life so remarkable was the handicap she endured and overcame—total blindness. At the age of just six months, treatment for an inflammation of her eyes blinded her for life. She could never see, but in a very poignant way she never looked back, either. Throughout her life, she inspired others with her hard work and personal initiative. She even learned to play the piano, organ, harp, and guitar, and became a respected soprano singer. She was popular as much for her perseverance in the face of a horrific obstacle as for the many good deeds she performed.

Fanny Crosby set a personal goal of bringing a million people to Christianity through her hymns. Whenever she wrote one, she prayed it would bring women and men to Christ, and she kept careful records of those reported to have been converted through her works. She also wrote four books of poetry and two best-selling autobiographies.

America is a country with a history of heroes, but it seems at times that we've forgotten more than we're producing these days. Maybe there's a connection there. If we forget our heroes, how can their examples serve as inspirations? Fanny Crosby is worth remembering not only for what she did but for the good her story can still do today.

September 20, 2012

The Decline of Trust in Government

With so much talk these days of scandal, incompetence, and failed programs, trust in government is on the ropes. To some people, this development is lamentable. They write articles about the need to "renew our faith in democratic institutions." But this may be a case where the general population is smarter than the pundits.

Polls testify to a fading faith in government. One from the American Enterprise Institute more than a decade ago showed that barely 20 percent of Americans "trust government in Washington to do what is right 'most of the time' or 'just about always.'" That figure was down from about three-quarters of Americans in 1963.

A September 2011 CNN poll found that only 15 percent of Americans said they trust the government in Washington to do what's right just about always or most of the time. Seventy-seven percent of people questioned said they trust the federal government only some of the time, and an additional 8 percent volunteered that they never trust the government to do what's right.

The steep decline in trust in government since the mid-1960s is actually proof that large numbers of Americans are awake and learning something. Politicians who promised the sky delivered the proverbial mess of pottage instead. Remember how hundreds of billions of tax dollars siphoned through Washington would solve poverty? The result would be laughable were it not so tragic. This is the same crowd that can't balance the federal budget and indeed, one half of the Congress (the Senate) hasn't even approved a budget in the last four years.

What's lamentable here is that too many politicians lie, cheat, steal, promise more than they intend to deliver, and otherwise misbehave. It is not lamentable that Americans lose faith in them when they do those things. It is laudable, because it is common sense being appropriately applied.

After all, what does it mean to "trust" someone or something? It means that the object of your trust has earned your respect and confidence through high standards of reliability, truthfulness, and performance. No one, not even government, should be trusted unless and until behavior justifies it.

In 1997, economist James Glassman cited the encouraging results of this poll question: "Which statement comes closer to your view: 'The government is responsible for the well-being of all its citizens and it has an obligation to help people when they are in trouble,' or 'People are responsible for their own well-being, and they have an obligation to take care of themselves when they are in trouble'?" In 1983, 43 percent of respondents replied that the government is responsible and 46 percent said people are responsible. In the 1997 poll, however, the results were 16 percent for government, 66 percent for people. Can you think of any reason why the percent for government might be any higher today? Me neither.

While people are trusting government less, they are learning to trust themselves more, and that is a refreshing development.

September 27, 2012

A President Who Spoke Sense

Who was the last U.S. President to write all of his own speeches and deliver more speeches than any of his predecessors? While serving in the White House, he also held a whopping 520 press conferences—eight per month—more than any President before or since.

The answer is Calvin Coolidge, who earned the nickname "Silent Cal" in spite of his prolific record at the podium. It was in social settings and parties when he tended to clam up. At a dinner event when journalist Dorothy Parker leaned over to Coolidge and said, "Mr. President, I have a bet with a friend that I can get you to say at least three words," he famously responded, "You lose!"

When Coolidge spoke, he made more sense than many of the men who have held the highest office in the land, especially the one who holds it now. What he said about taxes in his inaugural address in 1925 you'll never hear from Barack Obama: "I want the people of America to be able to work less for the government and more for themselves. I want them to have the rewards of their own industry. That is the chief meaning of freedom. Until we can re-establish a condition under which the earnings of the people can be kept by the people, we are bound to suffer a very distinct curtailment of our liberty."

The current President tells entrepreneurs, "You didn't build that," as he buys votes by expanding dependency on government. Contrast that with what Coolidge stood for, as expressed in this statement from his days as governor of Massachusetts: "In a free republic a great government is the product of a great people. They will look to themselves rather than government for success. The greatness of America lies around the hearthstone."

In the 1920s, with Coolidge's strong support, the top income-tax rate fell from 73 percent to 24 percent. Americans with the lowest incomes benefited even more when the rate at the other end fell from 4 percent to 0.5 percent.

Coolidge knew something today's tax hikers don't: incentives matter.

In 1924, Silent Cal asked a large audience, "If we had a tax whereby on the first working day the government took 5 percent of your wages, on the second day 10 percent, on the third day 20 percent, on the fourth day 30 percent, on the fifth day 50 percent, and on the sixth day 60 percent, how many of you would continue to work on the last two days of the week?"

In the years that Coolidge was vice president and then President, the economy grew by nearly 60 percent, the national debt was reduced by a quarter, and the federal budget was consistently in the black. If it hadn't been for the wrong-headed policies of the Federal Reserve and Presidents Hoover and Roosevelt, the Coolidge prosperity could have lasted through the 1930s.

I miss Calvin.

October 4, 2012

The Income Tax, 99 Years Later

I wrote this column before Wednesday night's presidential debate, but it's safe to assume that taxes—income taxes in particular—were part of the circus. Rates are set to rise painfully in January if Congress doesn't act beforehand, so we'll all be talking a lot about taxes in the next few months. A little history could be useful.

The federal income tax started small just 99 years ago (in 1913), but grew quickly in size and scope. The top rate was first set at a mere 7 percent, and married couples were only taxed on income over $4,000 (about $90,000 in today's dollars). During the tax debate, Congressman William Shelton of Georgia supported the income tax "because none of us here have $4,000 incomes, and somebody else will have to pay the tax." Sounds just like that famous line, "Don't tax you, don't tax me, tax that man behind the tree."

Some people scoffed at the notion that the income tax would ever take as much as 10 percent of anybody's money, but it took the politicians barely 20 years to sharply increase the rates and expand the base of those who had to pay it. Presidents Herbert Hoover and Franklin Roosevelt, using the excuses of depression and war, permanently enlarged the income tax. Under Hoover, the top rate was hiked from 24 to 63 percent. Under Roosevelt, the top rate was again raised—first to 79 percent and later to 90 percent.

In 1941, in fact, FDR proposed a 99.5 percent marginal rate on all incomes over $100,000. After that proposal failed, Roosevelt issued an executive order to tax all income over $25,000 at the rate of 100 percent. He also promoted the lowering of personal exemptions to only $600, a tactic that pushed most Americans onto the tax rolls. Congress rescinded Roosevelt's executive order, but it approved the personal exemption reduction.

The progressive income tax allows politicians to protect friends, to punish enemies, and to tax one small group to give benefits to larger targeted groups. In the 1920s, Sen. James Couzens of Michigan said, "Give me control of the Bureau of Internal Revenue, and I will run the politics of the country."

When President Nixon discussed who he wanted as Commissioner of Internal Revenue, he said, "I want to be sure that he is ruthless, that he will do what he is told, that every income-tax return I want to see, I see; that he will go after our enemies and not go after our friends. It's as simple as that."

Today, though rates are lower than their all-time highs, the paperwork is massive and incomprehensible. Add the value of the time we spend on filing it all and worrying that we got it right and you know why Ronald Reagan once defined what a taxpayer was this way: "Someone who works for the federal government but doesn't have to take the civil service examination."

October 18, 2012

Big Government Can't Possibly Be Good Government

It's a good bet that no matter where you are on the political spectrum—liberal, conservative, libertarian, or something else—you want men and women in government to be honest, humble, fair, wise, independent, responsible, incorruptible, mindful of the future, and respectful of others.

But you may be holding profoundly contradictory views without realizing it. This is the bottom line: The bigger government gets, the less likely it will attract men and women who possess those traits we all say we want.

Have you noticed how mean and nasty campaigns for high office have become? Lies and distortions are common political fare these days. Why would a genuinely good person subject himself to the ugliness of it all? Increasingly, genuinely good people don't bother, so we are left all too often with dirtbags and demagogues in government. Unless you enjoy rolling in the mud with the hogs, you stay on the other side of the fence.

There are reasons for this disturbing situation, and they have to do with the nature of power. Lord Acton famously stated more than a century ago that "Power corrupts, and absolute power corrupts absolutely." He nailed it, though I would add a corollary of my own: "Power attracts the corrupt."

If you've supported the monstrous expansion of the federal government in recent decades, or if you've got a laundry list of things you want it to do because you think it's not yet big enough, then don't blow smoke about clean and honest politics. You're part of the problem. Big government, by its very nature, is dirty and dishonest. That's the kind of people it attracts, and that's what concentrated power is always about.

America's founders had lots of reasons for wanting to keep government small, reasons the government schools rarely teach these days. One of those reasons was that they knew the wisdom of Lord Acton's warning a century before he wrote it. It would be inconceivable to our founders that good and honest people could ever stay good and honest if they're swiping and redistributing $4 trillion every year and regulating almost every corner of life. That kind of power can make a sinner from a saint in no time.

Think ahead to what all this means in the future if the federal government continues to grow unchecked. Some day when it controls 50 or 60 or 70 percent of national income, it'll be stuffed full of arrogant, manipulative, slick-talking but low-character types. They will not be people who are wise enough to realize that they're not smart enough to run everybody else's lives. Then when we realize we've put some of the worst among us in charge of a gargantuan machine, it'll be too late. Power attracts bad people, and bad people don't go away quietly.

Big government equals bad government. Don't fool yourself into thinking otherwise.

New Passport Form Wants Info on Your Mother

Did your mother receive medical care while pregnant with you and/or up to one year after your birth?

"It's none of your business," you're probably thinking—and you'd be right. But if the U.S. State Department has its way, you'll answer this very question or you may be denied a passport.

The department's proposed "Supplemental Questionnaire to Determine Entitlement for a U.S. Passport" (Form DS-5513) also wants to know who your mother's doctor was, what the dates of her appointments were, and who was present at the "birthing location." One line actually asks you to reveal the "length of time mother stayed at the birthing location listed above."

For most of our history, passports were not required for overseas travel at all. The Fourth Amendment to the Constitution unequivocally established "the right of the people to be secure in their persons, houses, papers and

effects against unreasonable searches and sei-
zures." Bureaucrats prying into your personal
affairs before giving you permission to travel
wouldn't have gone over very well.

Until 1941, the only times that passports
were required were during the Civil War, then
during World War I and for three years thereaf-
ter. In 1921, the Harding administration abol-
ished the requirement, but it reappeared in
1941 and has remained in place ever since.

From World War II until the "War on Terror,"
getting a passport didn't require much more
than a birth certificate and filling out a short,
relatively easy-to-complete form. The new
Form DS-5513 requests information that for
most people will be impossible to furnish. It
should make you wonder if the State Department really wants to give you a passport at all.

"Please provide the names (as well as address and phone number, if available) of persons present at your birth such as medical per-
sonnel, family members, etc.," the form asks. In
another place, it wants to know "any schools,
day care centers, or developmental programs
you attended from birth to age 18 in or outside
of the United States" as well as "all of your resi-
dences inside and outside of the United States
starting with your birth until age 18."

It might be tempting to dismiss this as the

product of some paper-pushing, low-level bureaucrat who is simply one neuron short of a synapse. But Form DS-5513 was first proposed in early 2011. After a firestorm of opposition, the one major revision the department made was to drop the question about whether you were circumcised and with what accompanying religious rituals. The department is now using the form even though it says it still is only "proposed." Requiring someone to complete it, according to Robert Wenzel in the *Economic Policy Journal*, "would amount to de facto denial of their application for a passport."

Barack Obama promised the release of information as part of "the most transparent administration" in history. Maybe what he had in mind was your information, not the government's.

Hurricane Sandy Was Not a Stimulus Project

It never fails. After every natural disaster (and even after devastating wars), somebody claims that the destruction is actually good news.

Hurricane Sandy was still wreaking havoc last week when John Silvia, chief economist for Wells Fargo, appeared on CNBC to proclaim the rebuilding effort in coming months would boost the economy. When the interviewer noted the reconstruction efforts after Japan's horrific tsunami produced disappointing economic numbers, Silvia said the situation in the northeastern United States was different because it's a wealthier area. People, businesses, and governments will now spend a lot of money to fix things up, he said, and that's a plus for the economy.

You're a better economist than Silvia if you're asking yourself, "Doesn't the spending to rebuild come from somewhere, and if we didn't have to spend to replace stuff, wouldn't we have that money for other uses?"

Why is it that so many people, including some prominent mainstream economists like Silvia, get sucked in by such utter nonsense? Why do they apparently think that it's a stimulus when other people's homes are destroyed but not their own?

It's hard to imagine survivors of the fire in Queens or the flooding in Atlantic City deriving much solace or consolation from Silvia's comment.

"I'm so glad my home was flattened because now I have the chance to rebuild it and stimulate the economy" is not a widely held view in the Northeast at the moment, I'm sure.

The "destruction is a blessing" folks are simply not thorough in their thinking. When a window in a home is broken, they see the new business the glassmaker gets but ignore the fact that the unfortunate homeowner now can't buy something else because he has to replace the window.

A French economist, Frédéric Bastiat, exploded this "broken window fallacy" 160 years ago, and you can read his classic essay at tinyurl.com/btkavec.

Wouldn't it be great if we lived in a world where destruction was indeed a magical route to economic progress? It's the one thing that governments do very well and have more experience in than any other group or institution. Blowing things up or tearing them down is a lot easier to accomplish than creating them in the first place—and for some, it can be downright fun as well. We could dispense with toil and sweat and just go on a rampage, knowing that the economy was being boosted in the process. If Mother Nature wouldn't cooperate by giving us an occasional disaster, we could blow up a few dams and create our own floods.

Hurricane Sandy was an unqualified disaster. Reconstruction spending will shift resources from this to that, from here to there, just to replace what people once had. Production, not destruction, makes an economy grow. Silvia should ask Brown University, where he earned his economics degree, for a refund.

November 22, 2012

Be Thankful Every Day

Thanksgiving is just one day of the year, but we have so much to be thankful for that maybe it should be the other way around: Make Thanksgiving every day but one. Then on that odd day, we can ask forgiveness for not expressing our gratitude.

G. K. Chesterton once said, "I would maintain that thanks are the highest form of thought; and that gratitude is happiness doubled by wonder."

Think about that, especially Chesterton's use of the word "wonder." It means "awe" or "amazement." The least thankful people tend to be those who are rarely awed or amazed, in spite of the extraordinary beauty, gifts, and achievements that envelope us.

A shortage of "wonder" is a source of considerable error and unhappiness in the world. What should astonish us all, some take for granted or even expect as an entitlement.

We're moved by great music. We enjoy an endless stream of labor-saving, life-enriching inventions. We're surrounded by abundance in markets for everything from food to shoes to books. We travel in hours to distances that required a month of discomfort for our recent ancestors.

In America, life expectancy at age 60 is up by about eight years since 1900, while life expectancy at birth has increased by an incredible 30 years. The top three causes of death in 1900 were pneumonia, tuberculosis, and diarrhea. Today, we live healthier lives and long enough to die mainly from illnesses (like heart disease and cancer) that are degenerative, aging-related problems.

Technology, communications, and transportation have all progressed so much in the last century that hardly a library in the world could document the stunning accomplishments. I still marvel every day that I can call a friend in China from my car or find the nearest coffee shop with an app on my iPhone. I'm in awe every time I take a coast-to-coast flight, while the unhappy guy next to me complains that the flight attendant doesn't have any ketchup for his omelet.

None of these things that should inspire wonderment were inevitable, automatic, or guaranteed. Almost all of them come our way by incentive, self-interest, and the profit motive—from people who gift their creativity to us not because they are ordered to, but because of the reward and sense of accomplishment they derive when they do.

Some see this and are amazed and grateful, happy and inspired. Others see it and are envious and unappreciative, angry and demanding.

Which are you? The answer may reveal whether you're a maker or a taker, a person who will leave the Earth a better place or a place that will regret you were ever here.

Leonard E. Read wrote a classic essay ("I, Pencil") in 1958 that explains the exquisite fact that no one person in the world knows how to make a simple pencil, yet pencils and far more complicated things are produced by the boat-load every day. (You can read it here: http://ti-nyurl.com/3pgfdys).

We should be thankful we have so many reasons to wonder.

November 26, 2012

Just Say No to the Marijuana War

The most potent mind-altering drug isn't one that you stick up your nose or inject into your arm. It's called the truth. In spite of your best efforts to sometimes keep it out, it tends to migrate straight to an important internal organ that biologists identify as the brain— but it can take a long time and a tortuous route to finally get there. The war on marijuana is a case in point.

Before you jump to conclusions, please note: I don't smoke the stuff, and I don't encourage anybody else to unless they derive some personal pleasure or medical benefit from it and don't harm anybody else when they do. I just don't believe the best way to deal with a popular plant involves cops, helicopters, raids, shoot-outs, and prisons. Marijuana has killed far fewer people than swimming pools; it's the war against it that does all the violence.

On November 6, voters in Colorado and Washington approved ballot measures legalizing marijuana for recreational use—the first such statewide votes in U.S. history. My first thought when I heard the news was a single word: Hallelujah! Maybe now, at least in those two states, more law enforcement resources can go toward crimes that actually have victims.

The evidence has been staring us in the face for years. Laws against the growing, possession, or use of marijuana have been a colossal and expensive failure. Anybody who wants it can get it, easily. The war against it is no more effective or desirable than alcohol. Prohibition was in the 1920s and early 1930s. Until we threw in the towel on that fiasco, we spent a fortune in a doomed and senseless effort to keep people from their booze, and we shot up the streets in the process. Organized crime was the biggest beneficiary because the cops were busy jailing the less fortunate competition.

Thanks largely to our marijuana laws, we prop up Mexican drug cartels with billions in artificial profits. The associated violence in Mexico on both sides of the border kills and maims thousands more in any one year than marijuana itself has in the last century. More than 40,000 people are languishing in jails and prisons right now on marijuana charges—virtually all of them nonviolent offenders—at an average annual cost of more than $20,000 each. What on earth do we have to show for all this stupidity? Nothing but pain and sorrow and diminishing public treasuries, not to mention the liberties we've lost because of property forfeiture and other intrusive police powers.

If we banned milk, we would produce precisely the same effects. The streets would be full of milk pushers. The milk business would go to the Al Capones of the world instead of to your local grocer. But anybody who wanted to drink milk and pay the price would get it anyway, right down the street next to the police station.

It would be charitable to say the war on marijuana is a failure or a futile effort. It's a human tragedy. Just say no to it.

A Good but Reluctant President

Why is it that the people who don't lust for public office tend to make better public servants if they attain it? That's my impression, admittedly not a carefully studied perspective. I'm more confident suggesting that those who *do* lust for office should be summarily rejected. If you enjoy power over others, I don't want you near it.

I recently enjoyed reading about a man who was as reluctant for power as any who have ever wielded it—James A. Garfield of Ohio, elected President of the United States in 1880. The book by Candice Millard is titled *Destiny of the Republic: A Tale of Madness, Medicine and the Murder of a President*. It focuses on Garfield and his eventual assassin, Charles Guiteau, mostly in the two years before the latter shot the President just four months into his term.

"This honor comes to me unsought," Garfield said. "I have never had the Presidential fever, not even for a day."

A former Civil War general, Garfield was a

48-year-old, nine-term congressman in 1880. He showed up at the Republican National Convention that year to place the name of Senator John Sherman in the hat for the party's presidential nomination. The other two candidates were Senator James G. Blaine of Maine and former President Ulysses S. Grant, who had come out of retirement to seek a third-term comeback.

Early in his speech, Garfield asked, "And now, gentlemen of the convention, what do we want?" Loudly from amidst the crowd came the unexpected reply, "We want Garfield!" It was a Saturday night in early June in Chicago.

The Sherman, Blaine, and Grant forces pressed for a vote shortly before midnight. The chairman refused to allow business to spill over into the Sabbath, so he recessed the convention until Monday morning. Garfield spent Sunday pleading with conventioneers not to vote for him.

On the third ballot on Monday, one vote surfaced for Garfield. Twelve hours later, Sherman, Blaine, and Grant were deadlocked short of the votes to win.

Tuesday morning the contest resumed. On the 34th ballot, Garfield's number rose to 17, prompting the noncandidate to leap to his feet in protest. The chairman cut Garfield off, gaveled him out of order, and told him to take his seat. On the 36th tally, as Garfield looked on in horror, he won the nomination.

Garfield was "shocked and sickened." He departed in a carriage, rode to his hotel in silence with "a grave and thoughtful expression on his face," and then collapsed in a chair looking "as pale as death." He won the general election in November.

As President, Garfield proved honest and competent, but he was appalled at the endless lines of people who wanted a favor or a job. "Almost everyone who comes to me wants something," he wrote. He later complained, "My God! What is there in this place that a man should ever want to get into it?"

Garfield's presidency lasted 200 days. For 80 of them he lay wounded from Guiteau's July 2 assassination attempt. He died on September 19, victim of a crazed man who *did* lust for public office and was angry that the President hadn't offered him one.

If not for a bullet, the man who least wanted to be President might have become known as one of our better ones.

The Brown Bomber vs. the Tax Man

D o you remember the most famous fight for the world heavyweight boxing title between Detroit's Joe Louis and Germany's Max Schmeling? If you do, you're getting up there in years. It was in 1938. It was a rematch that Louis, known as the "Brown Bomber," won in just 124 seconds.

Another fight that Louis waged is less well known. It was with the Internal Revenue Service. As we do in our day, Louis had to contend in his with a President whose fingers itched to get into the pockets of wealthy Americans. I first learned of this story from historian Burton Folsom, author of the superb books, *New Deal or Raw Deal?* and *FDR Goes to War.*

In 1935, President Roosevelt pushed Congress to raise the top income tax rate to 79 percent, then later to 90 percent during and after World War II. In the war years, Joe Louis donated money to military charities, but the complicated tax laws wouldn't allow him to deduct those gifts. Although Louis saw almost none of the money he won in charity fights, the IRS credited the full amounts as taxable income paid to Louis. He had even voluntarily paid back to the city of Detroit all the money he and his family had received in welfare years before but that counted for nothing with the feds.

Louis retired as heavyweight champion in 1948 but his tax debt was approaching $500,000. After an IRS ruling in 1950, the debt began accumulating interest each year. Louis felt compelled to come out of retirement in 1950 to fight Ezzard Charles, the new champion. After the fight, his mother begged him to stop, but, he said, "she couldn't understand how much money I owed. . . . The government wanted their money and I had to try to get it to them."

The next year, Louis fought Rocky Marciano and lost. The fight earned him $300,000. With a 90 percent tax rate, what he had left was peanuts, but he gave it all to the government. When his mother died in 1953, the IRS swiped the $667 she left him in her will. With interest compounding, his debt by 1960 had soared to more than a million dollars.

According to Folsom, "Louis refereed wrestling matches, made guest appearances on quiz shows and served as a greeter at Caesar's Palace in Las Vegas—anything to bring in money" for the IRS.

The notorious mobster Frank Lucas (still living today at 82) was so disgusted with the IRS treatment of Louis that he once paid a $50,000 tax lien against the boxer. Even Max Schmeling came to the rescue, assisting with money when Louis was alive and then paying funeral expenses when the boxer died in 1981.

Louis, a decorated Army veteran and athlete, remained a symbol of black achievement in spite of his tax troubles, which finally came to an end when the IRS settled. When Louis died, President Reagan waived the rules to allow for him to be buried in Arlington National Cemetery with full military honors. He was a hero in more ways than one.

February 7, 2013

The Quackery of Economic Equality

While equality before the law is a noble goal worth fighting for (indeed, many Americans have sacrificed both their lives and fortunes for it), equality in wealth is both dumb and unachievable. In purely economic terms, we should understand this fundamental truth: Free people are not equal, and equal people are not free.

Put another way, then, the statement might read, "Free people will earn different incomes. Where people have the same incomes, they cannot be free."

Free people are different people, so it should not come as a surprise that they earn different incomes. Our talents and abilities are not identical. We don't all work as hard. And even if we all were magically made equal in wealth tonight, we'd be unequal in the morning because some of us would spend it and some of us would save it.

To produce even a rough measure of economic equality, governments must issue the following orders and back them up with firing squads and prisons: "Don't excel or work harder than the next guy, don't come up with any new ideas, don't take any risks, and don't do anything differently from what you did yesterday." In other words, don't be human.

We should rejoice that free people don't earn equal incomes.

Economic inequality, when it derives from things like merit and free exchange and not from political power, testifies to the fact that people are being themselves—each putting his uniqueness to work in ways that are fulfilling to himself and of value to others.

People obsessed with economic equality do strange things. They become envious of others. They covet. They divide society into two piles: villains and victims. They spend far more time dragging someone else down than they do pulling themselves up. They're not fun to be around. And if they make it to a legislature, they can do real harm by passing dumb laws and jacking up taxes.

If economic inequality is an ailment, punishing effort and success is no cure in any event. Laws and taxes that aim to redistribute wealth prompt the smart or politically well-connected "haves" to seek refuge in havens here or abroad, while the hapless "have-nots" bear the full brunt of economic decline. A more productive expenditure of time would be to work to erase the many laws, orders, and ordinances that assure that the "have-nots" are also the "cannots."

Economic equality is neither possible nor desirable in a free society. We'd be so much better off if governments understood this basic truth, especially that really big, bloated one that sits in Washington.

February 14, 2013

The Power of Positive Example

Close your eyes for just a few seconds and think of one or two people who have motivated you, encouraged you, spurred you on. Then ask yourself, was it because of what they said, or what they did? How they talked, or how they behaved?

What those people did and how they behaved probably had the more lasting impact. Certainly, no one is inspired in a positive way by the hypocrite or by the unprincipled. To paraphrase Ralph Waldo Emerson, "What you are speaks so loudly I cannot hear what you're saying."

Each of us is inspired far more by the power of positive example than by commands or threats. Doesn't it mean so much more to us to earn the respect of others as opposed to commanding it? How much have we really won if others pay attention not because they want to but because they have to?

I can think of so many things I wish more people would do. I wish they would value education more highly and read to their children. I wish they would show more concern for those around them in need and do something about it themselves instead of waiting for the government to do it (at 10 times the price). I wish they would work harder at being the very best at whatever they've chosen as their life's work. I wish they would show more respect for the lives and property of others. I wish they would be better neighbors, more caring friends, more honest politicians, more responsible business associates.

We could pass laws that would force more people in these directions and that would penalize them if they failed to comply (Congress does it all the time). But that approach leaves me with a feeling of hollowness. I don't want a society in which people do the right thing just because they have to, when they really don't want to. And I believe strongly that the most effective but underappreciated teaching method is the power of positive example.

Forcing a person to go to church doesn't make him religious any more than forcing him to stand in a garage makes him a car. You don't make a person truly loyal by forbidding disagreement. You don't make a person charitable by robbing him at gunpoint and spending his money on good things.

What we sometimes forget in our haste to

reform the world is that we must first reform ourselves, one at a time, and none of us has yet done all we can in that regard. We chronically underestimate how much influence for good we can be by simply being better individuals— not pontificating about doing good, but actually being good—and doing it with our own resources, not someone else's.

Being as good as we know in our hearts we should be—in our speech, conduct, and relationships—is still the best advice any of us can either give or take.

March 11, 2013

The Jesse Jackson Lesson

If you marinate your kids in the wrong values as they're growing up, don't be surprised if they end up screwed up, or in jail, or both.

That's the sad lesson of former congressman Jesse Jackson, Jr., who last month agreed to plead guilty to charges of fraud, conspiracy, making false statements, mail fraud, wire fraud, and criminal forfeiture. He and his wife illegally sucked up about $750,000 in campaign money for personal expenses that included a Michael Jackson fedora, cashmere capes, a gold-plated Rolex watch, and Eddie Van Halen's guitar. They filed false income tax returns for the years 2006 to 2011, at the same time the hypocritical, left-wing power couple were denouncing rich people for not paying their "fair share."

I admit right up front that I'm not a psychiatrist. I don't know the Jackson family. But I'll bet my wisdom teeth (I still have them!) that Jackson's problems started in the home, decades ago.

It wasn't merit or character or any particular expertise that put Jackson in Congress in 1995. It was mainly his famous name and the connections handed to him by his father and the corrupt-to-the-core Chicago political machine. It's unlikely that brains played much of a role either. This is the same guy who proposed a couple years ago that every student in America receive an iPad from the federal government and then a month later blamed the iPad for "eliminating thousands of American jobs."

Like his father, Jackson loved wielding power. He was implicated, though not convicted, of shady dealings to buy a Senate seat from the crooked Illinois Gov. Rod Blagojevich, who is presently doing time at a Colorado penitentiary. When the Senate eluded his grasp, Jackson slumped into depression. He disappeared last year for months on end, then resigned his House seat in November.

If the apple never falls far from the tree, I think Jesse Sr. may have been an important reason for Jesse Jr.'s life path from power to prison.

Jesse Sr. did some good things early in life, but the example he has set for the past four decades is mainly that of a hustler, a demagogue, and a race-baiter. CNN revealed that he had his "nonprofit" Rainbow Push Coalition pay his mistress thousands of dollars to keep quiet. He owes much of his considerable personal wealth to scams, as documented in ace investigative reporter Kenneth R. Timmerman's 2003 book, *Shakedown*. If Jesse Jr. saw his father as a role model, then he learned early that lying, power-seeking, corruption, double-dealing, and cover-ups are the way to go in life. No wonder the son was attracted—and ultimately brought down—by an obsession for flashy, ego-satisfying, but ephemeral baubles like furs, cars, watches, and Senate seats.

It's fashionable in some places these days to sneer at "old-fashioned" values like hard work, personal character, and responsibility—especially if abandoning them buys you notoriety, wealth, and influence. But the fact remains that teaching and practicing those values won't ruin your life and put you behind bars.

About the Author

Lawrence W. ("Larry") Reed became president of FEE in 2008. Prior to that, he was a founder and president for twenty years of the Mackinac Center for Public Policy in Midland, Michigan. He also taught Economics full-time and chaired the Department of Economics at Northwood University in Michigan from 1977 to 1984.

He holds a B.A. degree in Economics from Grove City College (1975) and an M.A. degree in History from Slippery Rock State University (1978), both in Pennsylvania. He holds two honorary doctorates, one from Central Michigan University (Public Administration—1993) and Northwood University (Laws—2008).

A champion for liberty, Reed has authored over 1,000 newspaper columns and articles, dozens of articles in magazines and journals in the U. S. and abroad. His writings have appeared in The Wall Street Journal, Christian Science Monitor, USA Today, Baltimore Sun, Detroit News and Detroit Free Press, among many others. He has authored or co-authored five books, the most recent ones being "A Republic—If We Can Keep It" and "Striking the Root: Essays on

Liberty." He is frequently interviewed on radio talk shows and has appeared as a guest on numerous television programs, including those anchored by Judge Andrew Napolitano and John Stossel on FOX Business News.

Reed has delivered at least 75 speeches annually in the past 30 years—in virtually every state and dozens of countries from Bulgaria to China to Bolivia. His best-known lectures include "Seven Principles of Sound Policy" and "Great Myths of the Great Depression"—both of which have been translated into more than a dozen languages and distributed worldwide.

His interests in political and economic affairs have taken him as a freelance journalist to 81 countries on six continents. He is a member of the prestigious Mont Pelerin Society and an advisor to numerous organizations around the world. He served for 15 years as a member of the board (and one term as president) of the State Policy Network. His numerous recognitions include the "Champion of Freedom" award from the Mackinac Center for Public Policy and the "Distinguished Alumni" award from Grove City College.

He is a native of Pennsylvania and a 30-year resident of Michigan, and now resides in Newnan, Georgia.

FEE's mission is to inspire, educate and connect future leaders with the economic, ethical and legal principles of a free society.

For young minds interested in an introduction to free market economics and its foundations in the broader philosophy of individual liberty, FEE is the best source for inspiring content, programs and community. FEE is not an academic or political organization; instead our focus is making the economic, ethical and legal principles of a free society widely accessible, easily understood and energizing to young minds. We do this by delivering content that is substantive and thoughtful in forms most convenient to our customers, including in-person seminars and lectures, web-delivered content, printed material in book and magazine form, and networking opportunities. At FEE, young people—and educators who work with them— will find an exciting and optimistic introduction to the Austrian and classical liberal traditions in free market economics as well as opportunities to connect with other young people and free-market organizations around the world.

Made in the USA
Charleston, SC
17 July 2013